Follow Me On Instagram and Check Out My Amazon Store For Updates and My Latest Book Releases!

AUTHOR_CALEB_ELLIS

Follow me on Instagram using the QR code above.

Follow my Amazon store using the QR code above.

We Need Your Feedback:
Please Leave Your Amazing Review On Amazon!

This Book Belong To

____

Acknowledgement

To my beloved daughter Chloe, you are the inspiration behind my push to become a children's book author. I pray this book provides you with guidance on boundaries at this early stage in your life. Also, I extend my heartfelt gratitude to my family who encouraged me to keep publishing and pursing my dreams.

Lastly, a special acknowledgment to the wonderful students I've had the privilege to work with. Your stories, enthusiasm, and insights have significantly shaped this book and my perspective.

Hi, my name is Bella!
I've got a big topic to cover.

I'll share about boundaries.
Things I learned from my dad and mother.
Say NO!
1 Teach children the correct names for their body parts.
2 Explain that our private body parts are those under our bathing suit (also include the mouth).
3 Instruct that no one can touch your private body parts or show you pictures of private body parts.
4 Explain you must never touch another person's private body parts even if an older child or adult asks you to.
5 Discuss Early Warning Signs. i.e. sweaty palms, racing heart, sick tummy; always act on your early warning signs.
6 You can shout, "Stop" or "No!" (hand held out) if touched on your private body parts.
7 Tell a trusted adult straightaway if you are touched on your private body parts, shown pictures of private body parts, or your Early Warning Signs kick in.
8 Keep on telling until you are believed.
9 Never keep secrets that make you feel uncomfortable or unsafe.
10 Be strong, be brave and ALWAYS speak out!
12
9
3
6

Each person has a personal bubble.
An invisible space you can't see.

It's important to respect each bubble.
For everyone, even friends like me.

If you wonder what this bubble looks like,
lift your arms and move them front to side.

If you stand still while you're doing this,
your hands and nothing else will collide.

When you want to hug or touch someone, always ask them before you do.
YES!
Can I give you a hug?

"Can I give you a hug?" You ask.
The choice is up to them, not you.

If someone makes you uncomfortable with a touch or word they say.
Can I touch your hair?
Please stop!

You have the right to tell them, "Stop!" And quickly walk away.
That's him!
Reception

One time, my cousin kept tickling me.
It was really funny at first.

When I asked him to stop, he said okay. So my boundary bubble wouldn't burst.
Okay That's enough!

And what about your feelings? Well, they have boundaries too.
That is not my name.

SAFE TALK
AND
BOUNDARIES
Did you know that you can choose the way people talk to you?
Sorry!

There are parts of your body, that are private just for you.
private parts for Girls
private parts for Boys

You must guard those private areas,
in everything that you do.

No playing
There are certain places where,
boundaries must always stay.
The bathroom is that place,
that you should never ever play.

Go to the stall and use the bathroom.
That's what my dad would say.
Afterwards, wash your hands, then leave.
That is the proper way.
Exit

Also, remember about words. Not everything should be said.
That was stupid!

Think before you speak your mind,
Or you might hurt someone instead.
That hurt my feelings.

Listening is a boundary too.
When someone is sharing, give them space.

Let them talk and open up,
with a kind and understanding face.

Always remember to be respectful,
in all that you say and do.

Boundaries help us feel safe and loved,
for all, like me and you!

Boundaries Resources

Boundaries are like invisible rules that help us feel safe and happy. They are the lines we set for ourselves and others, so we all know what's okay and what's not. It's like having your own space where you decide what happens.

Physical Boundaries: These are about your body and personal space. For example, if you don't like being hugged by someone you don't know well, you can say, 'I don't want a hug, but I can give a high-five!' This is you setting a physical boundary. It's like having an invisible bubble around you, and you decide who can come into the bubble.

Verbal Boundaries: These have to do with the words we use and hear. If someone says something mean or uses words that make you uncomfortable, you can say, 'I don't like those words, please don't use them with me.' This is setting a verbal boundary. It's like having a rule about what kind of words are okay and not okay to say and hear.

4 Strategies To Manage Boundareis

1. **Speak Up:** If you don't like something, it's okay to say so. You can tell someone, "Please don't do that, I don't like it." Your words are powerful, and you have the right to use them to talk about your feelings.

2. **Listen to How You Feel:** Notice how you feel inside. If something makes you feel uncomfortable or unhappy, that's a sign. It's your body telling you something important. Remember, you can always say 'no' or walk away if you don't feel good about a situation.

3. **It's Okay to Say 'No':** Remember, saying 'no' is okay. If you don't want to play a game, share a toy, or be hugged, just say 'no, thank you'. You get to choose what you're comfortable with.

4. **Ask for Help:** If you're not sure about something or if someone isn't listening to your 'no', talk to an adult you trust. It can be your teacher, your parents, or any adult you feel safe with. They are there to help you.